MW00676611

The Aierdi Miracle

An Amazing Story of Providence

The Aierdi Miracle

An Amazing Story of Providence

ANDY BONIKOWSKY

Mauldin, South Carolina

CTS Publications, LLC

The Aierdi Miracle
Copyright © 2013 by Andy Bonikowsky

All rights reserved. No part of this publication may be reproduced, stored in a retrieval system, or transmitted in any form or by any means—electronic, mechanical, photocopy, recording, or any other—except for brief quotations in printed reviews, without the prior permission of the publisher.

All Scripture quotations, unless otherwise indicated, are taken from the Authorized King James Version.

Project Manager: Lauri Bayless
Cover design: Dwight Reid
Editor: Christina Gradwell

Printed in the United States of America

ISBN: 978-0-9886056-0-2
Library of Congress Control Number: 2013930019

12   11   10   9   8   7   6   5   4   3   2   1

Acknowledgements

A number of individuals and groups of people were essential to the publication of *THE AIERDI MIRACLE*. The desire to write the story was born very soon after it happened, but the Lord waited a dozen years to bring all the right circumstances together. One of the last pieces to slip into place came about through a comment made by my sister-in-law, Debbie Allen, when she told me about a friend who helped authors publish their books.

I tremble to think of what the final product would have been if the Lord had not brought Lauri Bayless across my path! From the establishing of CTS Publications LLC on through the numerous steps of editing, registering, and printing, she was not only professional and thorough, but a delight to work with. Thanks, Lauri!

Another friend who deserves special mention is Christina Gradwell, who years ago came to the mission field to help my wife teach our four children. Currently a busy pastor's wife and mother of five, she far exceeded our expectations when we asked her to help revise the draft. Thanks, Christina!

The Aierdi Miracle story is far more than just the initial facts set forth in this book. Today it continues on because of a wonderful missionary team that works together throughout the year. There would be little ministry going on at the farmhouse if it weren't for Juan & Tete Alvarez,

Randy & Karen Wilkins, Mike & Madelaine Dodgens, and Miss Sarah O'Brien. They help make the Aierdi experience a rich spiritual blessing to all who come. I am thankful for each one of you!

Finally, I could not possibly ignore the influence of my family in anything the Lord allows me to do. My wife Mimi, David, Danny, Mark, and Rachel, prayed with me all through this exciting journey. Together we had the priceless joy and privilege of watching God act before our eyes. I love you!

— Andy

Dedication

To three special men God has placed in my life —

Al Bonikowsky, my father. As far back as I can remember, he has been an example of quiet, unassuming faithfulness to the calling of God on his life.

Flay Allen, my father-in-law. Ever since I met him when I was a boy, he has been an example of constant and contagious joy in the Lord.

Dr. Danny Sweatt, my pastor. For over a dozen years he has been a source of wise and godly counsel as pastor of our sending church.

Table of Contents

Preface

It was shortly after dawn on a Thursday in the middle of July, 1996. We were four hours into the 440 mile trip from Madrid, Spain, to Bordeaux, France. I had borrowed a white Ford van from a fellow missionary because the Multilith 1250 printing press we were picking up would not fit in my minivan. On the passenger's side was a newly-arrived Mexican missionary to Spain, Juan Alvarez. The night before, as I visited the church whose pastor was lending me the van, I had explained to Juan the purpose of my trip. When he found out that I would be returning the van to Madrid as soon as I unloaded the press at our church in the Basque region, he asked if I wouldn't mind him coming along for the ride. I was glad to accept his offer, never suspecting that the next 16 hours of conversation would actually be the beginning of a wonderful missionary team.

The stars were no longer visible as we drove by the provincial capital of Vitoria and were forced to squint as the sun rose brilliantly before us. There, on the stretch of eastbound expressway that heads into the heart of Basque country, we shared family backgrounds and ministerial dreams. It was then I first heard about Juan's dream of being involved in a Christian retreat and conference center. When I heard his words they struck a chord in my heart … it sounded great! But wait. The idea was a bit too fantastic and a little far-fetched for a tiny ministry like the one into which God had called my family.

Neither of us realized that as we drove down the highway on that bright morning, Someone else was interested in our conversation. Far more than just a silent and invisible Listener, the very God of Abraham was bringing us together and calling us into an adventure that was grander and sweeter than anything we'd ever imagined.

Introduction

On the side of a mountain in the Basque region of northern Spain, an old rock building is quietly becoming a trophy to God's glory. Miles away from the noise of modern highways and towns, it perches on a gentle ridge at the end of a valley. The ancient farmhouse was built many generations ago by men whose names have been lost in the mist of unwritten history. Silently it watches as the events of days and months and years take the shape of a monument, a spiritual kind of monument. Bit by bit, a beautiful masterpiece is being sculpted.

God is carving out yet another unique witness to His timeless wisdom and almighty power.

If the Master were to give the aged walls permission to speak, they would undoubtedly tell of the profound change that has occurred in recent years. On the ground level, the bellowing of cows in dark stalls has been replaced by the happy chatter of children, youth and adults enjoying a meal in the attractive dining room. In the adjoining main entrance, where for centuries the matters of land and crops were discussed, Bible students, congregations, and mission teams today meet for prayer and song. Rooms that used to be living quarters for farm owners have disappeared and been replaced by dormitories, bathrooms, and a kitchen. The upper lofts, once crammed with bales of hay and farming equipment, now display rows of chairs where people of all ages and walks of life sit to hear the preaching of God's Word.

The transformation has been dramatic.

And how exactly did this come about? Was it the brilliant idea of some ambitious preacher? Did it come about through the endowment of some wealthy, charitable organization? Or could the secret lie in a marketing strategy that met with amazing success?

The answer is, "None of the above."

Rather, the Lord of heaven brought it about in His own creative way. First, He selected a beautiful setting, with an unused farmhouse, deep in the hills of the lush province of Gipuzkoa, Spain. Then, years before the prayers of His servants would begin to rise or any human mind had conceived the idea, He set in motion a series of events that were essential for it to happen. As He prepared the stage and put each of His children in place, God had to rearrange many things. Ministry plans were changed, doors were shut, dreams were squelched, and families were moved around.

But in His perfect time, each of the pieces was in place.

You will find this story to be one of puzzling disappointments, confusing delays, and exciting surprises. These are all intertwined perfectly to display the marvelous wisdom of God and His authority over every little detail of life. As you see the overwhelming evidence that the only real Hero of the events was the Lord, I trust you will be encouraged to trust Him more than ever. He delights in showing off His glory through normal people. God is not looking for spiritual heroes, nor does He need them. Rather, He usually seeks out the simple ones, young and old. They are individuals who have little that is attractive in themselves, but who are willing to step out in quiet and persistent faith.

Do you long to see the Lord do great and mighty things in your life? Have you thought His special favors were only for some highly qualified set of believers? I hope the following record of events will change your mind. What a joy it would be if this story stirs you to look to Him, call on Him, and believe in Him enough to wait for His response!

If you do, you will not be disappointed.

— Andy Bonikowsky
www.Aierdi.org

CHAPTER ONE

The Little White Card

*For my thoughts are not your thoughts,
neither are your ways my
ways, saith the Lord.*

~ *Isaiah* 55:8

The window was white with little cards, advertising everything from garages in town to summer apartments on the Mediterranean coast. As I stood looking over them in front of the real estate agency, one card caught my eye. It advertised the sale of a Basque farmhouse for $100,000 near a tiny mountain village called Zerain. For us, that might as well have been a million dollars! But we decided it would make a good prayer challenge for our upcoming furlough in the USA.

For months my co-worker, Juan Alvarez, and I had been considering the need for a ministry facility that could serve as a tool in our church planting ministry. A farmhouse like this advertised one might just be the perfect place. The first thing that came to mind was what a great location it would make for the printing equipment. We were already producing literature for churches all over Spain, but the growing printing ministry took up much-needed space in our small church building. And secondly, since people were so hesitant to visit an evangelical church, we thought a more neutral place, like one of their own farmhouses, might be excellent for outreach activities.

It was with this possibility in mind that we reported to our supporting churches in the fall of 1997. We asked people to pray for God to give us a Basque "caserío" (farmhouse) like the one I had seen offered on the little, white card.

God is Always Doing More Than You Think!

When we returned to Spain in December, I went to the agency and was elated to discover the farmhouse was still for sale. I immediately set up an appointment to meet the agent with whom I would discuss the condition of the farmhouse and the surrounding land.

It was in early January of 1998, over a cup of coffee at the Castillo Hotel Cafe, that I heard the sweet and sour facts. The good news was that the enormous two-story building came with approximately 65 acres of land. The view was breathtaking. From its windows you could watch flocks of sheep graze in the nearby pastures or lift your eyes over miles of forested hills to the faraway snow-covered

Txindoki mountain peak. But there was not-so-good news as well. First was the fact that the house had important deficiencies requiring major renovation. Then, there was a small portion of the building owned by another individual who was not willing to sell. And finally, the many acres of land were split up into several strips and sections so not all of the land surrounding the farmhouse came with it.

For this, the owners were asking the equivalent of $100,000.

In spite of these drawbacks, we decided to consider the proposition, believing the farmhouse still had great potential. My father, who was a builder before coming to the mission field, said he would be willing to tackle the construction part of it if we thought we could work around the other issues. That was encouraging, since without his talent and building expertise, it would not have been reasonable or possible to take the first step.

After facing these matters and deciding to go forward, we found ourselves before a daunting wall of questions.

How sure were we that God was behind this?

Where were we going to come up with $100,000?

Though we knew in theory that God could supply the money, would He do it for us?

Was this His project or just an impossible and unrealistic dream of our own?

One thing was very clear. We had no personal resources or influential contacts to lean on. We were going to need a miracle straight from Heaven! The only way we would end up with a farmhouse for the ministry would be through a miraculous intervention of God.

As it turned out, Heaven, or perhaps better expressed, "the heavens", would have a lot to do with the outcome of this story.

For as the heavens are higher than the earth, so are my ways higher than your ways, and my thoughts than your thoughts.
~ *Isaiah 55:9*

God Is Always Doing More Than You Think

Six years before the idea of purchasing a farmhouse ever crossed our minds, the Lord moved us away from the coast where we had planned to start a church. He guided us specifically to the interior Goierri region of 18 towns and directly to the tiny one called Zegama. His Spirit led us to exactly the right apartment, owned by a lady who was born and raised in the farmhouse God would give us years later. This was done against human logic, for the landlady had always refused to rent it, even to family and friends.

You may look around and think the circumstances of your life seem pretty random, dull, or insignificant. But if you are His child, Your life is on His mind and is important to Him. He wants to involve you in the grand work He is already doing within your circle of influence. However, He expects you to act by faith, believing Him to be active even now in the affairs that surround you.

CHAPTER TWO

Count The Stars

*And he brought him forth abroad, and said,
Look now toward heaven, and tell the stars, if
thou be able to number them: and he said unto
him, so shall thy seed be.*

~ *Genesis 15:5*

The opportunity was there. Quickly the enormity of the challenge began to shake our confidence. If God was in this, we needed special confirmation from the Lord. None of our missionary team had ever taken a step of faith quite like this before, and we were a bit nervous. I decided to write and ask advice from several ministry friends and family members.

All of them responded and encouraged us to go ahead.

One missionary suggested we notify our supporting churches and friends. This comment became the impetus that encouraged us to write a brochure to present the project. Others encouraged us to step out by faith, but only after we were sure it was God's will. These and other thought-provoking words fueled our desire to know God's will for sure before marching forward.

I was the one designated to write the brochure, so, on the second Sunday of January, I began to organize my thoughts and to write out the details of the project as we understood them. On Thursday I was back at the computer, again working on the text, and becoming more and more frustrated. By the time the town's church tower bell had rung its 12 midnight chimes, I was stumped.

There is Beauty in the Details

Something was missing.

What I had written so far didn't sound very convincing. I couldn't put my finger on it, but the text lacked a clear thought, a key phrase, a theme to tie it all together.

We needed a miracle from God and these sentences just were not communicating the urgency I felt in my heart.

I decided to read over the emails I had received during the previous weeks.

That simple decision was a providential nudge from the Holy Spirit. It was a tiny step that would lead us into His will, transforming our lives and bringing a whole new dimension of faith to our ministry. Yet it happened in the most ordinary way.

I began scanning over the printouts, like a kid looking for the right puzzle piece from the pile on the table.

One of those emails, from Dr. Mike Patterson, had only four lines and read, "When the price is within our means, when the way is within our view, when the solution is within our capacity, no faith is required. When the price, the way, and the solution are in God's hands, He can if He wants to. And if he doesn't, we are better off without it."

Then he signed off his brief note with the words, "Count the stars with Abraham."

Now that was odd …

Count the stars?

What on earth did *Count the Stars* that have to do with anything? Why in the world should I count the stars?

I began to think, as I made my way to Genesis, focusing in on the famous conversation between Abraham and Jehovah.

There I reviewed the story, quickly remembering that many years earlier the patriarch had been promised he would have a son. At the time of this conversation, the man called out from Ur of the Chaldees was old, confused, and frustrated. God had given him everything He had promised … except what he wanted most.

The promised son.

Now he was venting his frustration before the Lord with a bold and somewhat irritated attitude.

God's quick and blunt response seems to indicate that He was not going to tolerate any more complaining.

"Get outside and look up into the blackness on top of you."

"Now count the stars, if you can."

As Abraham lifted his eyes towards the dark canopy overhead, a beam of light shown down powerfully on his disappointed soul.

Suddenly, it dawned on him.

The God who placed those innumerable stars in space was still fully capable of giving him a son. The first miracle was no harder than the second.

His responsibility was to wait, and count, and wait, and trust.

And then it hit me, too.

We also needed a miracle ... and those same stars were still up there. God wanted us to take the challenge, too.

He wanted us to count the stars just like Abraham.

And that was exactly what we could ask friends to do with us. Count the stars and trust God to work the miracle.

This was the theme I had been searching for.

From that moment the brochure had direction. The ideas began to flow, and by 3am, I thought it was pretty much finished. My mind was in a whirl, and I could hardly understand my emotions. I was both excited and frightened. The following journal entries from that night show how the

So it is with anything God makes, whether a pebble, a tiger, a cedar, or a galaxy …

Or a story.

Your life is no exception. God is at work in the specifics of your life, including every person, every place, and every event He brings you to. You may have to take that by faith now, but one day heaven will make it clear.

CHAPTER THREE

Four or Three?

If thy presence go not with me, carry us not up hence.

~ Exodus 33:15

But the brochure was not quite right ... at least as far as God was concerned. I was sure He was impressing on my heart that there was a part of the plan that would not give Him all the glory He deserved.

So, as with Gideon's army long ago, He decided to whittle it down.

There were two aspects of the brochure that began to trouble me. The first was linked to the desire on my part to make sure the idea was God's project and not ours. As Moses faced the huge task of leading the Israelites to the Promised Land, he said to the Lord, "If thy presence go not with me, carry us not up hence." (Ex. 33:15) He wanted nothing to do with the adventure if God was not in it. The Lord gave him the confirmation he requested and rewarded him with His unquestionable presence and power. I also wanted the Lord's confirmation that He was leading us to incorporate a retreat and conference ministry into our church planting efforts.

The second element that contributed to a change in the pamphlet came through a favorite book of mine. Years earlier, I had started reading *Hudson Taylor's Spiritual Secret* each January. Because of this, my heart was presently being stirred by the example of that missionary's unusual life. As a young man, he had learned to "move man, through God, by prayer alone" (Taylor 1990) and for decades, he consistently saw the Almighty hear and specifically answer many prayers.

Could the Lord not answer our prayers for funds without requesting it of others? Was He not able to do the same as He had done for Hudson Taylor 150 years ago?

From these thoughts a specific plan began to emerge which would serve as a confirmation of God's will.

What if we never asked anybody to give to the project? If this was the Lord's will, and not just a whim of ours, would He not confirm that by providing all the money without our specifically requesting funds?

With these thoughts on my mind, I called our co-workers, Juan and Tete Alvarez, and asked them to join

Mimi and me for one last meeting before printing out the "Count the Stars" brochures.

At our kitchen table, in the middle of January, 1998, I shared my heart with Juan, Teté, and Mimi. The fourth point in the project flyer—the one in which we asked people to give—had been bothering me all day. If we really believed God heard our prayers and could do anything He wanted, would it not be reasonable to trust Him alone to move His people to give for the farmhouse? If the Lord did indeed supply the $90,000 through prayer alone, would it not be a clear indication that we were doing exactly what He wanted us to do?

The four of us were in total agreement, so the request to GIVE was scratched from the text. It was now a three point challenge.

PRAY with us. FAST with us. COUNT with us.

We also agreed that it would be wrong for us to go into any kind of debt for the farmhouse. Once again our conviction seemed best expressed in the writing of Hudson Taylor, "I could not think that God was poor, that He was short of resources, or unwilling to supply any want of whatever work ... that if there were lack of funds to carry on work, then to that degree, in that special development, or at that time, it could not be the work of God." (Taylor 1990)

This then would be the final stamp of approval for us, the conclusive evidence that the Lord was behind the project. He would bring in the funds through the prayers of His people without our making any specific request for them.

It was a Saturday night to remember—a night of beginnings, a night of faith. It was the night we stepped out to believe in God alone, to count the stars and trust. We bowed our heads in prayer and the project began.

We had no idea God Himself had marked the date.

For ever, O LORD,
thy word is settled in heaven.
~ Psalm 119:89

The Eternal Word of God Still Speaks

It is easy to say God's Word is eternal!

But what do we mean? Often we are thinking only of the Bible as it relates to our calendar, meaning no more than that the Holy Scriptures will never be destroyed.

However, while that is definitely true, it means much more. The awesome fact is that still today, those who follow hard after God will hear His voice speaking to them through His Word. Thousands of years ago Jehovah gave a command and promise to Abraham, regarding the stars in the sky. Down through the centuries, many believers have undoubtedly sensed the same order as given to them, and they started to count. They were not disappointed.

Among them are some missionaries in northern Spain who trusted Him for a farmhouse.

How about you? Have you heard His voice and seen Him come through for you? Have no doubts that He wants to speak to you and use you in His service for His glory. But maybe He still needs to get your attention.

Perhaps He is still waiting for you to honestly come into His secret place of fellowship. Whenever you do, be sure that He will know how to communicate to you through His eternal Book.

CHAPTER FOUR

300 Addresses

And he said unto him, I am the Lord that brought thee out of Ur of the Chaldees, to give thee this land to inherit it.

~ Genesis 15:7

The next few days were filled with excitement as we fed stacks of paper into our noisy inkjets. Those were the days before digital cameras, so we took a picture of the farm and had several hundred prints made. When both sides of the brochures were printed, we folded them and glued the picture on the front. Then they were stuffed into envelopes and mailed to nearly 300 addresses ... which was the total number of people and churches we knew.

Almost immediately friends and churches began to respond to the mailing, and we entered into one of the most intense periods of our lives. From all over, people began to write to us to assure us they were counting the stars too and praying with us for the farmhouse. Here and there one would write, "We are excited about what God will do and want to give an offering to help." Though we were praying for this to happen, we were still shocked when notes came in announcing gifts of $50 or $100 or $500 or even $1,000. For a while, news of donations came in almost daily. Emails were flying back and forth between us, our mission office, and a growing list of those who were assuring us of their prayers.

How sweet was our fellowship with the Lord during that time. One, two, and often three times a day we would stop to count the stars in our hearts and pray to God. On many evenings, we would walk up the hill behind our town to pray under the stars ... and even count some of them.

Why not? Was that not something we could do? It seemed quite Scriptural that God would ask us to do something so simple and uncomplicated, something even a young child could understand.

The times of fasting were filled with extra Bible reading and worship. Through all of this, He was teaching us to pray, to depend on Him, to stand daily on His promise in Genesis 15:5. In a real sense we were putting our reputation on the line, risking failure and embarrassment if it all came crashing down into nothing.

God's Will May Include Waypoints

The following paragraph from a book I was reading seemed to apply:

Daniel and his friends were men who stuck their necks out. This was not foolhardiness. They knew what they were doing. They had counted the cost. They had measured the risk. They were well aware what the outcome of their actions would be unless God miraculously intervened, as in fact He did. (Packer 1973)

When the 15th of February arrived, gifts were still flowing in, but the total was not quite $9,000. To us that was a fortune, but it was very much short of the $90,000. God had not performed the miracle we had hoped for. There was no choice but to make the call and let the agency know we did not yet have the money, which meant the farmhouse would go back on the market.

It was time to call another team meeting.

*The steps of a good man are ordered by the Lord:
and he delighteth in his way.*

~ *Psalm* 37:23

What You Understand To Be God's Ultimate Will For You May, In Fact, Just Be A Waypoint.

Sometimes we jump to conclusions as we try to discern God's will.

For example, the Lord may lay some burden on your heart. You understand the direction He wants you to go and take off eagerly, with clear ideas as to what will happen and how things will be when you arrive at the goal.

But along the way things change. Unexpected events throw your entire program out of whack and suddenly your dreams go up in a puff of smoke.

You then sit down, dazed and confused, wondering what in the world happened.

Usually the problem is not so much one of following God's leading as it is understanding that He has a higher and fuller view of things. Often He will lead us in one direction for a while, to accomplish some phase of growth, or specific ministry. Once it is accomplished, He charts a new course, which we may mistakenly see as a change in plans.

This can be frustrating and perplexing if we do not realize what is happening.

Have you ever wondered at the seemingly random turns your path has taken? Maybe they were unsettling and left you bewildered and disturbed. It will help to remind yourself that you can leave the entire trip to the Lord, understanding that the destination immediately in front of you may actually be just a temporary stop along the way.

CHAPTER FIVE

Surprises

> *For every one that asketh receiveth . . .*
>
> ~ *Matthew 7:8a*

Now what?

It was with puzzled hearts that we met after church on Sunday night. As we talked it over, we concluded that God had brought in nearly $9,000 as a sign we were going in the right direction. But for some reason, it was not yet the correct time.

The tremendous pressure and intensity of the previous 30 days were over, and though that was somewhat of a relief,

The Bible is Full of Surprises!

we now faced the uncertainty of an indefinite wait.

Fortunately, as the prophet Jeremiah learned in prison 25 centuries earlier, the Lord loves to surprise!

"Call unto me, and I will answer thee, and shew thee great and mighty things, which thou knowest not." (Jeremiah 33:3)

These words came to a man who had received a very odd command from God.

Jerusalem, surrounded by the Babylonian army, was slowly being choked to death. Total destruction seemed like the only way it could end. Inside this groaning city was an inner court where the unpopular prophet was being held prisoner. It was here the Lord revealed to him that he would receive a visit from his cousin Hanamel, who would make him a very strange proposition.

The unusual offer was that Jeremiah consider buying a property in the town of Anathoth, three miles outside the city. What? Why, the Chaldeans were probably camping on it at that very moment.

It was such a peculiar request that when his relative showed up and spoke exactly as the Lord had foretold, Jeremiah had no doubt what to do. It was obvious Jehovah was fully in charge of everything that was happening. So without hesitation, he paid the seventeen shekels for the property.

Jeremiah received this timeless promise as part of his reward: Call on me and I will show you things beyond your dreams.

Perhaps the Lord, who loves to surprise, had some timely surprises around the corner for us too.

And He sure did! The day after that meeting, our mission office informed us that a man from Greenville had sent in $860 for the farmhouse. Later on the same day, a supporting pastor let us know his church had taken up a $1,050 offering for the project. The following day another church, with which we had had no previous contact, notified us they were sending in $2,000.

This was God's way of saying, "Don't stop praying. Don't stop fasting. Don't stop counting."

A string of gifts kept coming in for days until the total was over $15,000.

Then on February 26th, we received a disturbing call from the agency. There was another person seriously interested in acquiring the farmhouse.

Call unto me, and I will answer thee, and shew thee great and mighty things which thou knowest not.

~ Jeremiah 33:3

God Loves to Surprise!

The Bible is full of surprises. Both miracles and random events were constantly catching people off guard.

As we scan the stories of Scripture, we might find ourselves scratching our heads at the variety of the unusual ways of God. A multitude walks through the Red Sea. The sun stands still to lengthen a battle. A prophet receives his meals from a flock of ravens. A young man kills a champion giant with a sling. Three Hebrew boys walk around in a roaring furnace. An elderly statesman sleeps with hungry lions. A brave fisherman walks on water. I'm sure you have a few favorites I didn't mention.

A quick scan of history confirms that God has not changed. Down through the years He has filled the book of Christian biographies with an incalculable array of surprising experiences. With each one God shows off new facets of His wisdom and authority. He seems to throw each mold away and come up with a totally fresh scenario to display His glory.

We should expect this to hold true even in the tiny world of our personal lives.

Here is a suggestion that may really help you during one of those dreary days when it seems God has abandoned you. Start a list of the unique blessings God brings into your life. If you keep at it, it will grow through the years to become a powerful confirmation and register that the Lord is watching over you.

CHAPTER SIX

The Brochure Picture

He is thy praise, and he is thy God, that
hath done for thee these great and
terrible things, which thine eyes have seen.

~ Deuteronomy 10:21

It is no fun to wait.

We were now in the month of April, and the total amount of funds in the CTS account was over $20,000.

Weeks earlier, I had started reading Genesis 15:5 every day. Morning after morning I read the words of this verse until they were engraved on my heart. It just seemed like the right thing for me to do. Of course, I could soon quote it, but there was something special about opening the Scriptures and letting my eyes focus again and again on those words spoken to Abraham,

> *Look now toward heaven, and tell the stars, if*
> *thou be able to number them: and he said unto*
> *him, So shall thy seed be.*

That simple tradition began to grow as the Lord added more verses to my personal list. Deuteronomy 10:21 came alongside the initial verse, and then Psalm 27:14 joined them. This last verse reads,

> *Wait on the LORD: be of good courage, and he shall strengthen thine heart: wait, I say, on the LORD.*

During that spring of 1998, this verse became a constant companion, especially after a sobering thought crossed my mind. Since we were claiming God's promise to Abraham, what if we were going to be called on to wait for the same length of time he did? As I worked out the numbers the results hit hard. The patriarch was 75 when the Lord first told him of the promised son. He was 100 when Isaac was born. Would we also have to wait 25 years? Or more importantly, were we willing to wait 25 years?

With the daily repetition, the meaning of this verse began to sink in. Contrary to human logic, waiting was actually a good thing. Instead of weakening the heart, as one might expect, God promised to strengthen it. This was an important lesson to learn, especially when halfway through April another bit of news knocked us for a spin.

The Zerain farmhouse, for which we had been praying so diligently, the one on the picture glued on the front of every CTS brochure we'd sent out … had been sold to somebody else.

"I have labored in vain" is what Isaiah said in 49:4. This seemed to describe our situation perfectly. But God gave me strength to write in prayer,

> *I delight in your Word, Lord. It is my anchor. LORD, I look to you and trust. I have no answers, mostly questions.*
> *But my faith is in You. Help me to be an example of humility and confidence.*

Expect to Wait!

Again … now what?!

The four of us met again to try to figure out what to do next. One call and suddenly the whole scenario was different. Behind yesterday's mountain-size challenge to pray for the needed funds now towered a new and higher peak.

With $23,000 in the project account, it seemed obvious God had touched many hearts to give. But apparently the Zerain farmhouse was not His choice. The only conclusion we could come up with was that He wanted us to start looking for another place.

Ironically, the project now returned to being a four point challenge:

PRAY. FAST. COUNT. And now, SEARCH!

The problem was that there were very few farmhouses for sale and even fewer having the characteristics we needed for ministry.

And so God took us to a new level in the "waiting school" as He added a new assignment to our homework. Our prayer project was now expanded as we were faced with the added challenge of searching and finding the farmhouse of God's choice. He had shuffled everything around now and changed a major part of the project. It was as if He was redefining things so He would receive the glory more clearly. All we could do now was wait to see what He wanted to do. A journal entry on April 17th reflects some of this with the words,

Waiting on God purifies us of our self-sufficiency and underlines our need for Him. If what we expect does not come and we are forced to wait, we are forced to recognize our need for the Lord. This is good medicine for the heart.

Thankfully, God gave our many CTS project friends the loyalty to continue with us in the new challenge. Their faithful intercession and encouragement contributed to the outcome in a way we could never have anticipated.

Wait on the Lord: be of good courage, and he shall strengthen thine heart: wait, I say, on the Lord.

~ *Psalm 27:14*

You Can Expect to Wait

Waiting goes against our nature, which is to find the best life and enjoy it as soon and as much as possible.

But we see in the Bible that God often went to great lengths to make His children wait. Abraham waited for 25 years for his promised son. Moses watched sheep in the desert for 40 years. David ran for many months from murderous Saul. Paul spent a long time in Arabia, and then Tarsus, before starting his missionary ministries.

As we stepped out to trust the Lord for a farmhouse facility, we did not realize how long He would have us wait. It was necessary though, and as the search and prayer efforts dragged on, we began to understand the meaning of Psalm 27:14.

Wait on the Lord.

The ironic reality is exactly what the verse says. When we wait on the Lord, with the right attitude, our hearts are strengthened to believe Him more. The end result is stronger faith, not weaker.

Are you waiting on God right now? Do you have prayer requests you have been repeating to Him for years, or even decades? If so, be sure that this is absolutely normal. It is part of the Lord's program for every one of His disciples.

CHAPTER SEVEN

A Prophet Speaks

*And the word of the Lord came unto
me, saying . . .*
~ Ezekiel 34:1

We began searching on May 11th, 1998, praying to God for guidance, even in how to start. We decided that our first step would be to generally let it be known we were looking for a farmhouse for sale anywhere in the Basque region. A prayer journal entry read,

> *LORD, today we will begin to look for a farmhouse, and I hardly know where to start. We pray for guidance as we simply begin to ask questions. I have no idea how long it will take to find it. It is in Your hands. But I also wonder how people will give to the project, if we do not even have a farmhouse chosen. We must look to You, believing You have brought us to this point, and You know exactly where You are leading us.*

Juan and I followed up on every lead we heard of in our province of Gipuzkoa. Then we visited sites in the neighboring provinces of Navarra and Alava. We soon found out there were a number of obstacles we had never even anticipated. Not only were prices far more than the $25,800 now in the CTS account, but there were many other factors that eliminated farmhouses from being valid options for us.

For example, on several occasions we saw farmhouses that were built in deep valleys and hardly received any sunlight during the winter months. Once we drove up to a nice looking farmhouse that was clearly divided into two equal parts. One half was neatly painted and maintained, while the other was shabby and abandoned. We discovered that the two siblings who owned them had not talked to each other in 13 years … and of course, only one wanted to sell. On another occasion we followed a real estate agent to a farm that was on such a steep incline we couldn't see where to put even a small parking lot.

God's Will— Superior to Your Expectations

It became clear to us that everything we were seeing within our price range had major drawbacks and had to be ruled out.

Situations like these again highlighted the need for God's guidance and provision and made us read the Scriptures with continued alertness. Perhaps it was this heightened sense of need that made even the difficult writings of Ezekiel come alive with encouragement and direction.

One Saturday I was reading in Ezekiel 34 when God spoke to my heart as clearly, it seemed, as if He had whispered into my ear. Verse 14 said, *"I will feed them in a good pasture, and upon the high mountains of Israel shall their fold be, and in a rich pasture shall they feed upon the mountains of Israel."* I stopped immediately as thoughts rushed in loud and clear. Here was a promise from God concerning the farmhouse! The distance between the ancient context and our immediate need was spanned in a second as the Holy Spirit applied the Word.

Though the focus of the verse was on the nation of Israel, I saw in it three distinct features I believed were describing the farmhouse God had chosen, wherever it was. First, the word "pasture" meant it would have fields suitable for parking and outdoor activities of all kinds. Second, the "high mountains" meant it would not be down in a dark and damp valley like several we had seen. And finally, the "fold" meant there would actually be a farmhouse structure on the property. This last matter was significant because there were almost no options for construction permits on land that had no previous building.

These three criteria then became the litmus test for any site we checked out.

We soon realized that, one after another, the farms we visited failed to meet the threefold test. It wasn't long until there were no more properties to see and our efforts to find God's farm petered out.

There were simply no more farmhouses for sale.

Delight thyself also in the LORD; and he shall give thee the desires of thine heart.

~ Psalm 37:4

Dashed Expectations Do Not Mean The End Of God's Will

We have a tendency to run wild with our expectations, building entire castles out of flimsy dreams that are more our will than God's. At other times we may actually have the right idea in mind, but our timing is all off.

This happened to us several times in the CTS project, as we built our hopes on farmhouses and barns, only to have them implode when the properties were bought by other people. Even when we finally found God's choice, it was snatched away from us until the perfect moment He had chosen.

The mature Christian has so surrendered his will to his Master that he can honestly say, "*Whatever my Lord decides is fine with me!*" Before that can happen though, there has to be a deep learning experience in the character of God. This kind of attitude can only develop after the heart becomes convinced the Lord always selects the eternally best choice for His children. Once that is settled, the believer can wholeheartedly jump out of the boat to walk on the miraculous surface that leads closer to Jesus.

Have you ever had your expectations shredded? It is never fun. But hopefully, as you look back on the experience, you are able to accept what happened as God's perfect adjustment to your path. Slowly, as you see Him come through over and over again, your level of trust will bring you to delight in whatever our Lord chooses.

Ultimately, His plan for you will prove to be far superior to any expectations you ever had.

CHAPTER EIGHT

Silence

*Wait on the Lord: be of good courage,
and he shall strengthen thine heart:
wait, I say, on the Lord.*

~ *Psalm* 27:14

All went silent.

There was nothing to write about. Daily we prayed, and counted, and trusted, and hoped, but there was no exciting news to report. Correspondence diminished, gifts all but stopped coming in, we wrote fewer newsletters, and weeks went by with no apparent movement.

We were five months into the project, and now it all seemed to grind to a halt. It would be six months before the silence was broken. Here are some journal entries describing those perplexing times, even as we remained convinced that God had not forgotten us.

June 2, 1998—*Juan and I went land hunting today, but didn't find anything promising. We are running out of trails to investigate and things* *don't look very easy. But we are sure God has a place somewhere, and we need to keep looking until He guides us to it.*

June 11, 1998—*My Savior, what about land for a camp site? Will You give us a beautiful place up in the mountains with pastureland like Ezekiel speaks of? It seems almost impossible here. But You have done so much already. I look forward to more miracles from Your hand.*

June 16, 1998—*We must enjoy each phase of the CTS project. If we are always anxiously awaiting the next stage we will not be content with our experiences now. If we're not careful we can become impatient to know the place, and lose our joy. Later we will remember these times and talk about how good they were, but it would be better to remember actually enjoying the experience. We should enjoy exactly where we are if we are in His will.*

June 28, 1998—*One of the blessings of this method of praying [reading the verses as I pray] is that part of it is listening to God. It is not just my talking to Him, but listening as well.*

August 3, 1998—*I come to You, Lord, with Your Bible open to the promises You have given me. They are Yours, not mine. I have not scrounged them up, rather You have brought them to me as*

I've read. Now, I pray upon them for the needs.

August 12, 1998—*It is not only waiting we are called to do. Sometimes we have no choice! But He calls on us to wait happily in Him. That is a sign of faith.*

August 14, 1998—*Even as Psalm 27:14 tells me waiting is good heart medicine, so reading the verse and meditating on it daily is like taking the medicine in pill form. Lord, I long to see if I have understood Ezekiel 34:14 correctly. I wonder if I really hear the Spirit's voice in this matter. Time will tell.*

August 23, 1998—*Lord, this past week was completely silent on the project front. How hard at times to leave the whole matter entirely in the realm of prayer.*

August 31, 1998—*I'm in the van on a lonely mountain road. Both leads I followed to possible farmhouses were wild goose chases. I have absolutely no hope of finding a place based on what people say and the situation as I see it. There are almost no places for sale and many people are out looking for them just like me. I could not have a more hopeless situation. My only hope is in the promise God gave us. It will take a miracle straight from heaven for us to find a suitable place for the printing and camp ministries.*

September 2, 1998—*Ezekiel 34:14. When God gives us the place of His choice, the wait will have been worth it. It always is, for His will is best, even if it is much different than our dreams.*

September 9, 1998—*Last night I counted some stars from the balcony and [when I went in] God had the news of new gifts waiting for me on the computer. How happy I am that we are not asking people for money. Those who give, give because they feel led to give.*

September 29, 1998—*My Lord, I stand upon Your Book and its promises. You will not fail to fulfill what You have promised. I worship You for that and will wait happily for You to work Your plan.*

October 4, 1998—*The Lord has called on me to count the stars. Will I count or will I reason?*

October 5, 1998—*God has called upon us to do the impossible—count the stars. He is in the process of showing us just how impossible it is.*

October 16, 1998—*The stars say, "Hang in there, the Lord cannot fail you!"*

October 26, 1998—*The older Abraham got, the more "impossible" it was to have a child. So, the longer we take to find a farmhouse, the harder it will be. There is more and more of a* *demand and prices are on their way out of this world. Ours will have to be a miracle of God.*

October 31, 1998—*Ezekiel 34:14. I look forward to the day when we will see our Basque converts feeding themselves spiritually on the high mountains of this country, at the campsite God will give us. What a day of shouting that will be. But if Christ comes back, and it never happens? Who will complain?*

November 2, 1998—*I am really looking for the place described in Ezekiel 34:14. I think I will know it when I see it.*

CHAPTER NINE

The Borda Options

I wait for the Lord, my soul doth wait, and in his word do I hope. My soul waiteth for the Lord more than they that watch for the morning: I say, more than they that watch for the morning.

~ *Psalm 130:5, 6*

In the winter of 1998 we heard of a couple of options that sounded very promising. Two different "bordas" (Basque barns) were for sale in nearby valleys. They were not perfect in all aspects, but these bordas had two things in common: They were selling for roughly the $30,000 we had in savings, and both fit the characteristics of Ezekiel 34:14. Both had plenty of open land for activities, both were on the side of the mountain, with spectacular views of the Goierri valleys and peaks, and both included a building, or at least parts of one.

On the negative side, both were located far away from any road, with such difficult access they required the use of four wheel drive vehicles. There was a building on one of these locations which could barely qualify as a barn any more, having a caved in roof and walls that were only partially standing.

But they were available and within our means.

Or so we thought.

By this time, some readers may logically be asking why

God's Tool— Silence!

in the world we didn't just buy land and build from scratch. Actually, that would have been the easiest way to go about it and exactly what my dad would have preferred.

But the zoning laws in the Basque region prohibit most building permits outside of urban areas. Only through a very complicated process of developing the land for agriculture could a person eventually present a case for needing a barn or house on any property purchased outside town limits.

It was not unusual for the wealthy to buy land, build their fancy house on it, and then pay the fine if they were ever caught.

We figured that was NOT the way to start a Christian ministry. So, buying land and building on it was out of the question.

At any rate, when these two old barn possibilities surfaced, the oddest thing happened.

Though we had the money and were ready to buy from owners who wanted to sell, the Lord would not let it happen. We talked with the owners, went over plans together, and twice began the process of purchasing the properties. But a combination of paperwork problems and legal matters kept snagging the negotiations until finally we just gave up on both options.

For some reason, God did not want either of these bordas.

And once again, everything went quiet.

To every thing there is a season, and a time to every purpose under the heaven. . . . a time to keep silence, and a time to speak.

~ *Ecclesiastes 3:1, 7*

Silence Is One Of The Lord's Common Tools

Silence can be frightening and downright disconcerting, especially when it is on God's side. When people or machines are silent we can usually discover the reason, or simply accept it. But when all things go silent from heaven's direction, our blood chills and our thoughts run wild.

What have we done? Where has He gone? Why do we not hear from Him?

These questions are natural and needed. At times the answer will immediately come to us, and it may include some divine response to sin on our part. But then again, it may not have anything to do with our failure.

Job cried out intensely when it seemed like there was no communication from heaven. The various psalmists often penned the spiritual perplexities they felt when God was silent. And even prophets, like Habakkuk, turned their puzzled hearts towards the sky when prayers to Jehovah went unanswered.

In all three of these cases, the silence they experienced was not an expression of divine displeasure. Rather, it was part of the momentary agenda God had for their specific need and situation.

Have you gone through tunnels when there seemed to be no possible contact between you and the Lord? Do not interpret them as callous indifference on His part, nor careless negligence in guiding you through times of trouble. He may temporarily be quiet to your call, but He is never blind or indifferent to your need.

During the silence continue faithful in His Word, with complete assurance that sooner or later He will clearly speak to you again.

CHAPTER TEN

Ezekiel's Farmhouse

He staggered not at the promise of God through unbelief; but was strong in faith, giving glory to God; And being fully persuaded that, what he had promised, he was able also to perform.

~ Romans 4:20, 21

One day in early 1999, we heard about a farm for sale about a mile up the valley behind our town of Zegama. Since on an occasional Sunday afternoon we had gone near it on family walks, the news caught my attention. The property was known locally by the Basque surname "Aierdi", and what I remembered of the place was positive. I decided to check it out.

When I arrived at the green gate at the entrance to its land and looked up through the trees, I was shocked.

I was staring at a perfect image of Ezekiel 34:14! Resting on the east side of the mountain was an old rock farmhouse. The grassy slopes around it were perfectly positioned to welcome the sun each morning as it peaked over the facing hills.

Side of the mountain … farmhouse … grassy slopes.

I found a good spot, opened my Bible to Ezekiel 34:14, and pulled out my camera. In the lower part of the picture was the Scripture passage that was so clear. In the upper half of the photo was the farmhouse on the hillside.

Our search was over.

And that is exactly what I communicated to our circle of CTS praying friends. **We had found God's farmhouse!**

There was not the slightest doubt in my mind that this was the place chosen for us by the Lord of Abraham.

But there was one tiny problem.

Another man from town had just put down a reservation fee of $5,000 while he negotiated the financing. He had until March 24th to come up with the full amount.

The God of Abraham Chooses!

But that did not worry me. Wasn't this God's choice? He was able to overturn this person's plans, one way or another. In fact, it was going to be quite the adventure to watch it happen!

Out went the emails with the details of the prayer request. Once again scores of friends in stateside churches were earnestly praying. After so much waiting, finally, God had come through. Or at least, it seemed like it.

But how would He go about solving this new problem?

We had no idea, but we were sure it would happen.

In the coming weeks, we would be fasting, praying, and counting with fresh zeal, full of confidence and gratitude that God had moved at last.

It helped to find out from chit chat around town that the man who had put down the reservation money could not possibly have the resources. Most seemed sure he would lose his shirt. We weren't exactly praying for disaster to strike him, but we sure were hoping something would happen to make him back out of it.

On March 24th, I received a phone call.

The journal entry reads, "*Aierdi sold this morning. I am tired of the ups and downs. I am tired of writing people about it. I am tired of asking people to pray. I'm just tired.*"

In a little Basque village a very confused missionary tried to sort out his thoughts.

How could I have been such a fool? Why had I been so dogmatic? What on earth was I doing, trying to teach people how to determine God's will while making such a blunder myself? I determined never to stick my neck out like that again.

But by the grace of God, we did not quit.

Though stunned at the sudden turn of events, I kept on opening my Bible every day to Genesis 15:5, Deuteronomy 10:21, Psalm 27:14, Ezekiel 34:14, and Romans 4:20-21.

After all, the stars were still shining and we could still count.

Meanwhile, the new owner brought in heavy earth moving equipment and began to rearrange the landscape around the farmhouse, the one we had thought was God's. The sight of all the activity was so painful I decided never again to walk back up that road. It brought back unpleasant memories.

CHAPTER ELEVEN

The Coffee Maker

*For every one
that asketh receiveth; and he that
seeketh findeth . . .*

~ *Matthew 7:8a*

Seven months later nothing had changed.

We still counted the stars. We still asked God to lead us to His farmhouse. I still opened my Bible to my five good friends, the inspired words that kept our hopes alive.

One day a friend stopped me on the street below our apartment. He told me of an acquaintance of his whose job was to clean out buildings that had been repossessed by banks. This person had happened to mention to my friend about a café he was cleaning out up on the coast in the capital city of San Sebastian. During the conversation my friend had learned about an Italian espresso coffee maker that was going to be hauled off to the garbage bin.

Since he knew I liked coffee, he thought of me. "Would I be interested in a top-of-the-line coffee maker?"

"Of course!" I said immediately, "Some day, God will give us a farmhouse, and we will enjoy sharing the Gospel over a cup of coffee with unsaved friends who come to visit."

But there was a condition, one I wasn't eager to accept.

Nobody Can Guide Like God

We had to make arrangements to meet up with this guy. I didn't know him or where the café was, and it was quite a drive anyway.

I backed out. It wasn't worth the hassle.

This friend of mine, however, would not take "no" for an answer. He kept on insisting that it sounded like a good deal. Finally, to get him off my back, I agreed. I called Dad, who lived on the other side of the province, to see if he was interested in driving into the capital to meet me.

He was, so in mid-October, Mimi, our daughter Rachel, and I drove in to meet Dad at this abandoned café.

The man was there waiting. After introducing ourselves, we helped him raise the metal roll-up gate. The five of us walked right in through the showcase window which was broken. The place was dark and uninviting. The man had suggested we bring flashlights, and we now turned them on to see our way past the rows of tables and bar chairs.

As we walked beside the typical Spanish bar, we could not help but see the dirty plates and glasses and silverware, left on the tables as if everyone had fled in an emergency.

We shined the light at the large, dark object bolted to the wooden bar. It was the coffee maker all right. Electrical wiring, drainage pipes, and water tubes spread out into the darkness beneath the surface ... there were cobwebs and utensils ... who knows how long it had been there unused. It was filthy and speckled with rust.

It was a piece of junk.

"Sorry, Dad. What a waste of time. I didn't want to come in the first place."

I thanked the man for taking his time to meet us but told him we were not interested in the machine.

"Hey, look around to see if there is anything you can use," he said. "It will all be out on the street by Friday, and I've salvaged everything I can use. You can have anything that's left."

So we started looking.

After a few minutes I went back to the man. "Did you say anything we want?"

He nodded, "Anything."

We saw tables, chairs, plates, platters, pitchers, silverware.

Then we went up a flight of stairs leading to a second floor.

I came back down and went to him again. "Did you mean ANYTHING we want?"

He grinned, "Anything you can get out of here by Friday, you can have."

On the second level we had found a small restaurant, with its corresponding kitchen.

There was a stainless steel, triple burner stove, a 6ft X 6ft fridge, and tables. All of it was coated with nasty grease, but of course, one hard wipe of a finger revealed the shine of stainless steel. But that was not all. There were boxes of new coffee mugs, saucers, and plates. There were even fire extinguishers and brand new plumbing supplies.

We could hardly believe it.

A few days later we rented a small truck for about $20 and crammed it with the "spoil." There was so much stuff, we had to store it in three different places: the church building, our garage, and a friend's warehouse. As I drove towards the interior of the province, a thought came to me:

"God has just given us a kitchen, but we don't have a 'kitchen' to put it in!"

CHAPTER TWELVE

The Phone Call

I will feed them in a good pasture, and upon the high mountains of Israel shall their fold be: there shall they lie in a good fold, and in a fat pasture shall they feed upon the mountains of Israel.

~ Ezekiel 34:14

Four days later, in the evening, I received a phone call.

I heard the voice of an elderly gentleman, introducing himself as one of my father's uncles. I did not remember him specifically, but did recall being on his farm in Saskatchewan when I was a young boy. Our family was on furlough from Spain when we made the visit, and my only memory was of my dad letting me practice driving in the huge driveway in front of his home.

His reason for calling was to check out something. He had heard that we were praying for a piece of property for the ministry. He and his wife were recently retired and had some money they wanted to invest in the Lord's work. This was part of his investigation into several possibilities, and he was interested in knowing the facts firsthand.

I told him everything that had happened up until that night. He said they would be praying and would contact us again.

On November 2nd, I saw a newspaper clipping giving information about a farmhouse that was selling for roughly $112,000. As I read the description, it hit me. This was the property up the hill behind our town, *the building and land I had been sure was God's choice*. Remember the green gate, the sunny hillside, and the old farmhouse? It was the site a very confused and humbled missionary had walked away from seven months earlier. It was the place with the structure ... the view ... the land.

It was the Ezekiel 34:14 farmhouse.

God Uses His Own Calendar

It did not matter that after negotiating with the agency, the final price was $100,000, still over three times what we had on hand.

When "Uncle Bill" called the next week I had some exciting news to give him! He was very interested in the place and listened carefully as I described it and explained more clearly how it had once elevated our hopes.

When I finished he spoke so simply that the exact words still ring in my ears today, "Andy, my wife and I want to buy you the farmhouse."

What could I say? I was stunned. I hardly knew how to respond.

In fact, the first thing out of my mouth was, "We don't really need that much. We already have about $30,000."

Uncle Bill said that from what I had told him about the conditions of the ancient farmhouse, we would need a lot more than what we had to develop it into a useful ministry property. He then asked if there was any way we could reserve the place, because his money was not going to be available until December. I replied that it would be no problem to use some of the funds we had on hand to get a reservation contract in effect until then. When I got off the phone, I called Mimi.

"Honey, you are not going to believe what I just heard."

And he changeth the times and the seasons: he removeth kings, and setteth up kings.

~ *Daniel 2:21a*

God Uses His Own Calendar

The Lord pays attention to days and hours and minutes in ways that are invisible to us.

The Jews in Egypt were not looking at the calendar, but Jehovah was. The day they stepped out towards the Promised Land was undoubtedly very exciting, but mainly because of the terrific context in which it all happened. But God had His eye on the date, and specifically recorded it as being 430 years, to the day, after Jacob arrived with his family to meet Pharaoh.

Gehazi and the king, in 2 Kings 8:5, had no idea that God was synchronizing their conversation with the arrival of the Shunammite. Belshazzar the Chaldean and Darius the Mede were oblivious to the fact that a massive and blasphemous party inside the walls was coinciding perfectly with the date of the invasion.

But God did.

In your life as a child of the King there are no random events either. Your heavenly Father knows exactly how to orchestrate the activities that involve you according to an invisible calendar that only He can see.

Don't let the Devil trick you into thinking that God has lost sight of you and you have dropped off of His agenda. He has not changed one bit from Biblical times and that means He enjoys bringing glory to Himself as He manipulates dates and times. Arranging divine appointments is His specialty!

CHAPTER THIRTEEN

Made To Wait

Wait on the LORD, and keep his way, and he shall exalt thee to inherit the land: when the wicked are cut off, thou shalt see it.

~ Psalm 37:34

The people at the agency were happy to accept a token sum and give us a contract that held the farmhouse and land for us. When we went in with the $5,000, I noticed that the document gave us three months to come up with the rest of the money. This would take us clear into January of 2000. I told them there *God Said, "Wait!"* was no need for the reservation to be that long, because come early December, we would call them immediately to finalize the purchase. But for some reason they thought it was the correct procedure, so it stayed that way.

December came and a huge check in Canadian dollars was sent.

And it was lost.

Day after day went by as we waited and prayed and wondered. The check had not been certified, which caused some concern. However, it was duly cancelled and another check was sent, this time with all due precautions.

As the month wore on, the fact that the funds had to go from Canadian dollars to American dollars and finally into Spanish pesetas created a bit of nervousness … especially as much was being speculated over the potential effects of an electronic mirage called Y2K. Fortunately, all went smoothly. The turn of the millennium did not create worldwide, catastrophic computer damage nor did it affect the precious monetary gift we were expecting.

At any rate, the funds showed up in our Spanish bank on December 30th, and we slept soundly on New Year's Eve.

Well, we were eager to get this over with. But the next day was the last day of the year, and there was no way to get an appointment with the agency. New Year's fell on Saturday, so we would have to wait until the following week.

Bright and early on Monday the 3rd, I drove to the office in the capital to find out what was needed to sign the papers on the farmhouse. The person handling this particular sale was not there, and they told me to return the next day.

On Tuesday, to my consternation, they scheduled the signing for Thursday of the following week.

After all this waiting, and even with the money in hand, we were still having to be patient.

Early the next week, I got a call. Somebody in the office was sick and we needed to reschedule the signing.

Good grief! Now I was really beginning to wonder what was going on.

The person on the other end said, "Let's set the signing for the evening of the following Monday, January 17."

"What? That's the last day of the reservation contract we signed back in October. What if we have a snow storm and can't drive into the capital? Will we lose the $5,000 we gave up front?"

"No," they said. "Relax. There will be no problem. Just show up at the office at 8pm and we'll get it done."

Relax? That was easy for her.

I was not very happy.

But there wasn't much I could do about it, except leave it in the Lord's hands and trust Him.

The meeting at 8pm on January 17th turned out to be rather boring actually. Dad went with me and we walked into a room in which there were a number of men around the tables, lawyers and such. I never did quite figure out why they were all there. But the lawyer in charge insisted on reading slowly through bunches of official paragraphs detailing the transaction.

Finally, we handed over our paperwork, shook hands, and left.

CHAPTER FOURTEEN

At The Right Moment

And the LORD appeared unto Abram, and said, Unto thy seed will I give this land: and there builded he an altar unto the LORD, who appeared unto him.

~ *Genesis 12:7*

That was it.

The farmhouse was ours!

The Lord had paid for it in full. We had purchased it with cash and had never asked for money. Over the past couple of years our Bibles had been opened hundreds of times to Abraham's promise, and it was read and applied and believed. The CTS project was over.

Paid In Full

Or at least this phase of it.

But as I turned my car towards the mountainous interior on that dark January night, questions were swirling around in my mind ... questions that were begging for answers.

I had the sensation that more had just happened than we realized, that there was some specific reason why we had been delayed over and over again.

- Why had Uncle Bill's money not been available at the same time as the farmhouse?
- Why had that check been lost?
- Why had it taken so long for the second check to be processed?
- Why had the appointment been rescheduled twice?
- Why was the staff individual sick?
- Why had the signing date been shoved back and back and back until that Monday night?

There had to be a reason for all of these setbacks.

I decided to check my journals when I got home. Maybe through them the Lord would show me something and set my mind at ease.

I climbed the stairs to our third floor apartment and continued on up to the attic. In a matter of minutes I had located the journals going back to the first months of the CTS project. Soon I was reviewing the entries. I found references to our return from furlough, the white card farmhouse, the letter written to various men of God, the decision to look for a farmhouse, the writing of the brochure, the meeting to launch the project ... and then the following paragraph.

"So, last night we started printing out brochures. We eliminated the call to GIVE, wanting God's Spirit to do that work."

That was the night the four of us had met in our kitchen to launch the Count the Stars prayer project. How little did we understand that God Himself was present, orchestrating even the very date of the little prayer meeting. The journal entry indicated that the meeting around our table on that particular evening had occurred on January 17th, 1998.

It was then we had prayed and agreed not to ask people to give funds nor go into debt, as our way of knowing it was God's project.

The signing earlier this evening had taken place exactly two years later, to the day … and possibly to the very hour.

Only God can do that.

This is why we call the Aierdi building "God's farmhouse."

CHAPTER FIFTEEN

A New Step

And Moses called Bezaleel and Aholiab, and every wise hearted man, in whose heart the Lord had put wisdom, even every one whose heart stirred him up to come unto the work to do it.

~ Exodus 36:2

Now that the CTS project was over and the Aierdi farmhouse was ours, the next step seemed like an easy one. We would prepare another brochure to send all our friends, announcing the exciting developments and asking them to help us rebuild and develop the property into a ministry facility. It was quite clear that without a huge investment of outside funds, talents, and time, it would take us decades to get the place into any useable condition.

New Step of Faith

But the Lord blocked this plan.

Though it seemed like the most logical thing to do, I had no peace about it. After wrestling with the idea for several weeks, I finally came to understand what it was the Lord had in mind.

And He gave it to me through another verse.

Exodus 36:2 says,

> *And Moses called Bezaleel and Aholiab, and every wise hearted man, in whose heart the LORD had put wisdom, even every one whose heart stirred him up to come unto the work to do it.*

The Lord wanted us to take a new step of faith, one that seemed even scarier than counting the stars and trusting Him for the farmhouse.

He did not want us to ask anyone to come help with the work. Rather, He wanted us to pray and to trust Him to stir workers and send them to us.

Four months went by, months in which we brought in 84 tons of gravel for the driveway up to the house, and little else. Inside Aierdi very little had been done. With piles of clutter in the farmhouse, and very unstable flooring, when summer arrived the interior had hardly been touched.

Then one day in July I received an odd request. A group of nearly 30 Swiss believers were coming through our area on their way to central Spain for a retreat. We had met one of the young men a year before, and it had been his idea to ask us if they could spend the night on their trip south. They had tents and food and would be on their way the next morning.

Of course we were happy to let them come, so in mid-July they arrived at the property.

As soon as the vans had parked, some of the girls began to prepare a meal while a number of guys set up the tents. The leader of the group then asked if there was any work they could do for us.

A little while later a whole bunch of them were scattered throughout the farmhouse, hauling out tons of junk, tearing down old plaster walls, and generally clearing away sections of the old dwelling place. There was so much dust that many of them wrapped their faces with towels as makeshift filters.

At the end of the day they asked if we wouldn't mind them staying another day to continue working.

Then it dawned on us what was happening.

Exodus 36:2 was beginning to be fulfilled before our eyes.

God had surprised us again.

On the following day as the group was getting ready to leave, we gave them a little token of our appreciation. Each one received a bookmark, with the text of the above verse, and a number unique to them. It was the number of worker they were, having been stirred by the Lord to come to His farmhouse.

Thirteen years later the Lord is still sending workers to help.

In October of 2012 we hosted a mission team with more than a dozen adults from a church near Atlanta, Georgia, and of course, each one received a bookmark.

The numbers were 530-543.

Oh yes, do you remember the stainless steel kitchen equipment referred to in the Coffee Maker story? What do you think we have used to prepare the food for these hundreds of workers God has sent our way? You got it … He makes no mistakes!

So what is the lesson?

When we allow the Lord to do things His way, He receives the glory and we get to watch it happen. One of the exciting ways to have our faith strengthened is through personally seeing the wisdom and power of God in action. That is why waiting on God and being strong are so often linked together in the Bible.

Too often we rush ahead with our own ideas, too busy and too distracted to hear the still, small voice of God saying,

> *Wait on the LORD: be of good courage, and He shall strengthen thine heart: wait, I say, on the LORD.*

How about reading that verse again with fresh understanding that it is a message from God specifically for you?

But grow in grace, and in the knowledge of our Lord and Saviour Jesus Christ. To him be glory both now and for ever. Amen.

~ 2 Peter 3:18

God Wants Us To Grow In New Steps Of Faith

As long as we are in this body, God expects us to be growing.

The biologists tell us that we are slowly dying from the first days after our birth. Now while that is probably true physically, it is not the case with our souls. The Lord said our house of dust would return to the dust, but our spirit would go back to Him, to live on forever.

This would be reason enough to conclude that in this life we should never stop growing in Christ. Our ascent into the realms of our spiritual inheritance should be an ever rising spiral of Christian experience.

How exciting to see believers who are always alive with the fresh joy of Biblical discovery! They seem always to be finding new illustrations and applications of truth to stimulate their minds. They have an unquenchable thirst for the Bible and for the surprising challenges of faith it stirs up.

That is why we should never camp for long at the spot where we have just seen the glorious hand of God. Undoubtedly, in heaven we will have time for relaxation and reminiscing over victory stories. But this life is for stepping on, for moving forward, for growing further in our walk with the Master.

Don't ever be content to pull out the lawn chair, put your hands behind your head, stretch out your legs, and bask in the comfortable feeling of triumph.

At least, don't do it for long. There is so much more to conquer through the power of faith!

Scripture References

Genesis 12:7—And the LORD appeared unto Abram, and said, Unto thy seed will I give this land: and there builded he an altar unto the LORD, who appeared unto him.

Genesis 15:5—And he brought him forth abroad, and said, Look now toward heaven, and tell the stars, if thou be able to number them: and he said unto him, so shall thy seed be.

Genesis 15:7—And he said unto him, I am the Lord that brought thee out of Ur of the Chaldees, to give thee this land to inherit it.

Exodus 33:15—If thy presence go not with me, carry us not up hence.

Exodus 36:2—And Moses called Bezaleel and Aholiab, and every wise hearted man, in whose heart the Lord had put wisdom, even every one whose heart stirred him up to come unto the work to do it.

Deuteronomy 10:21—He is thy praise, and he is thy God, that hath done for thee these great and terrible things, which thine eyes have seen.

Psalm 27:14—Wait on the Lord: be of good courage, and he shall strengthen thine heart: wait, I say, on the Lord.

Psalm 37:4—Delight thyself also in the LORD; and he shall give thee the desires of thine heart.

Psalm 37:23—The steps of a good man are ordered by the Lord: and he delighteth in his way.

Psalm 37:34—Wait on the LORD, and keep his way, and he shall exalt thee to inherit the land: when the wicked are cut off, thou shalt see it.

Psalm 119:89—For ever, O LORD, thy word is settled in heaven.

Psalm 130:5, 6—I wait for the Lord, my soul doth wait, and in his word do I hope. My soul waiteth for the Lord more than they that watch for the morning: I say, more than they that watch for the morning.

Ecclesiastes 3:1, 7—To every thing there is a season, and a time to every purpose under the heaven.... a time to keep silence, and a time to speak.

Isaiah 49:4—Then I said, I have laboured in vain, I have spent my strength for nought, and in vain: yet surely my judgment is with the Lord, and my work with my God.

Isaiah 55:8—For my thoughts are not your thoughts, neither are your ways my ways, declares the Lord.

Isaiah 55:9—For as the heavens are higher than the earth, so are my ways higher than your ways, and my thoughts than your thoughts.

Jeremiah 33:3—Call unto me, and I will answer thee, and shew thee great and mighty things which thou knowest not.

Ezekiel 34:1—And the word of the Lord came unto me, saying,

Ezekiel 34:14—I will feed them in a good pasture, and upon the high mountains of Israel shall their fold be: there shall they lie in a good fold, and in a fat pasture shall they feed upon the mountains of Israel.

Daniel 2:21a—And he changeth the times and the seasons: he removeth kings, and setteth up kings.

Matthew 6:28, 29—And why take ye thought for raiment? Consider the lilies of the field, how they grow; they toil not, neither do they spin: And yet I say unto you, That even Solomon in all his glory was not arrayed like one of these.

Matthew 7:8a— For every one that asketh receiveth; and he that seeketh findeth ...

Romans 4:20, 21— He staggered not at the promise of God through unbelief; but was strong in faith, giving glory to God; And being fully persuaded that, what he had promised, he was able also to perform.

2 Peter 3:18—But grow in grace, and [in] the knowledge of our Lord and Saviour Jesus Christ. To him [be] glory both now and for ever. Amen.

Works Cited

Packer, J.I. 1973. *Knowing God,* Copyright (c) 1973 Used by permission of InterVarsity Press, PO Box 1400, Downers Grove, IL 60515. www.ivpress.com.

Taylor, Howard. 1990. *Hudson Taylor's Spiritual Secret,* (Moody Publishers), p. 32, 82.

CPSIA information can be obtained
at www.ICGtesting.com
Printed in the USA
FSHW021112151119
64083FS